This handwriting practice workbook
belongs to:

New Day
PRESS

Dear Sir (yes, I'm talking to you because this is a book written for sirs),

We realize that there are probably a million things you'd rather be doing than practicing your handwriting. We get it. It can be really dull.

But we also believe that having neat, readable handwriting is a valuable tool. Imagine you're all grown up and married one day and you leave a note for your wife to pick up some ice cream and hamburgers on her way home. Unfortunately, your handwriting is impossible to read, so she comes home with ice cubes and hominy. What a disappointment!

To help you out, we've tried to give you a fun break after each writing exercise to help you get your muscles moving and give your fingers a break. You may do all three pages for each letter and then take an Action Break or you could take an Action Break after EACH of the three pages for the letter. Take as many action breaks as you need to make the lessons fun and helpful. Our motto is, "Get the job done, and then have some fun!"

At the end of the book, you'll find some number practices, as well. Feel free to go back and choose any Action Break you like when you're working on numbers.

Wishing you great success and legible handwriting with lots of ice cream and hamburgers in your future!

arc arc arc arc

ar

ask ask ask ask

as

apple   apple

ap

ant ant ant ant

an

An astronaut

acts like an

ape in the alley.

write it on
your own

An

ac

ap

more
practice

Take a break!

Letter **A** Actions

Act like an ape.

Arch your back like a cat.

Act like an anteater.

buddy   buddy

bu

bad   bad   bad

ba

best   best   best

be

brown   brown

br

Boys bounce
balls on lumpy,
bumpy beds.

write it on
your own

Bo

ba

bu

more
practice

Take a break!

Letter B Actions

Bend down and touch your toes.

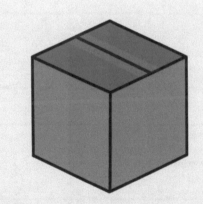

Beat on a box with your hands.

Bounce a ball.

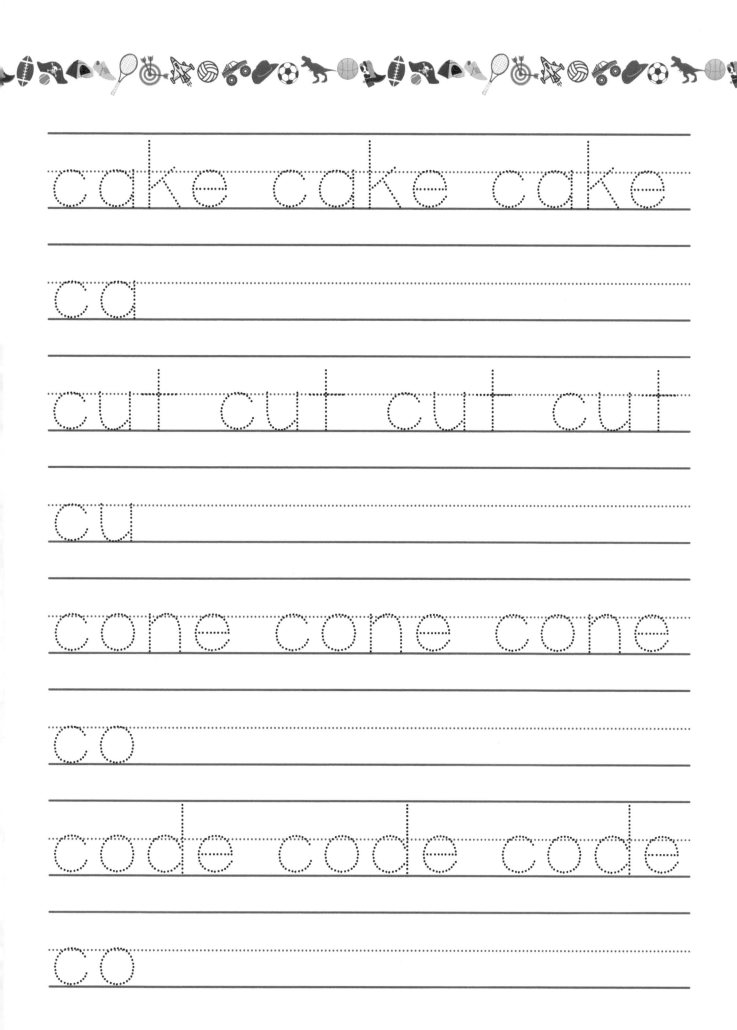

cake cake cake

ca

cut cut cut cut

cu

cone cone cone

co

code code code

co

Cats cook
cauliflower and
cookies.

write it on
your own

Ca

ca

Co

more
practice

Take a break!

Letter C Actions

Crawl around the room like a bug.

Carry an armful of pillows across the room.

Creep like a caterpillar.

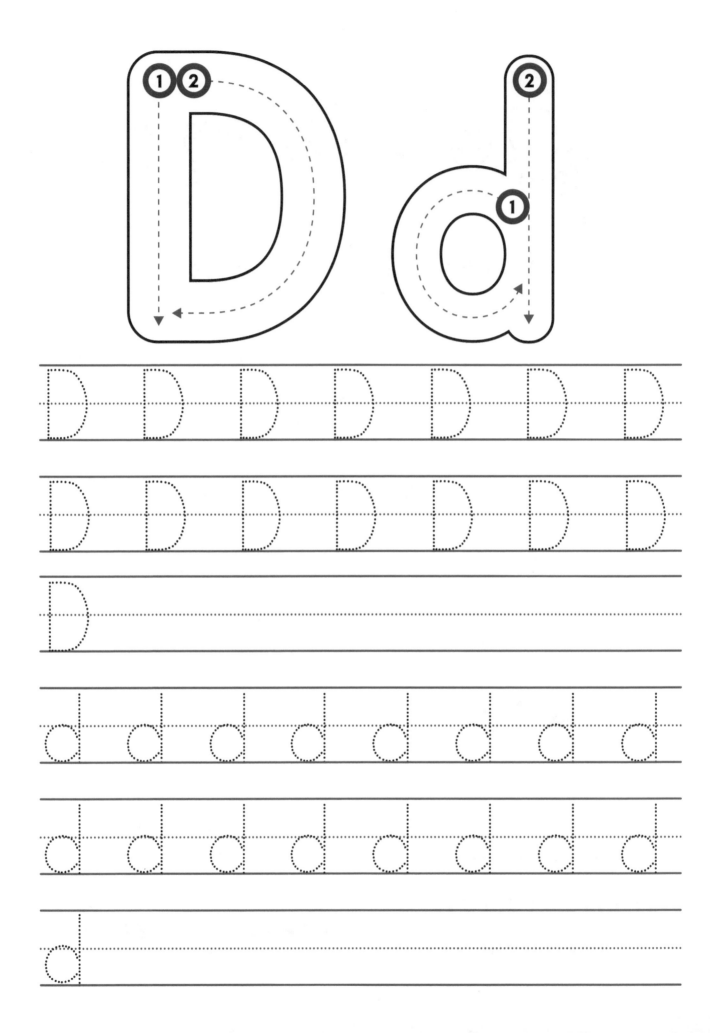

dig dig dig dig

di

dump   dump

du

dust dust dust

du

dark dark dark

da

Dogs dance downstairs with dopey dinosaurs.

write it on
your own

Do

da

wi

di

Take a break!

Letter D Actions

Drop something and pick it up again 10 times.

Dance all around the room.

Defend your stuffed animals like a knight.

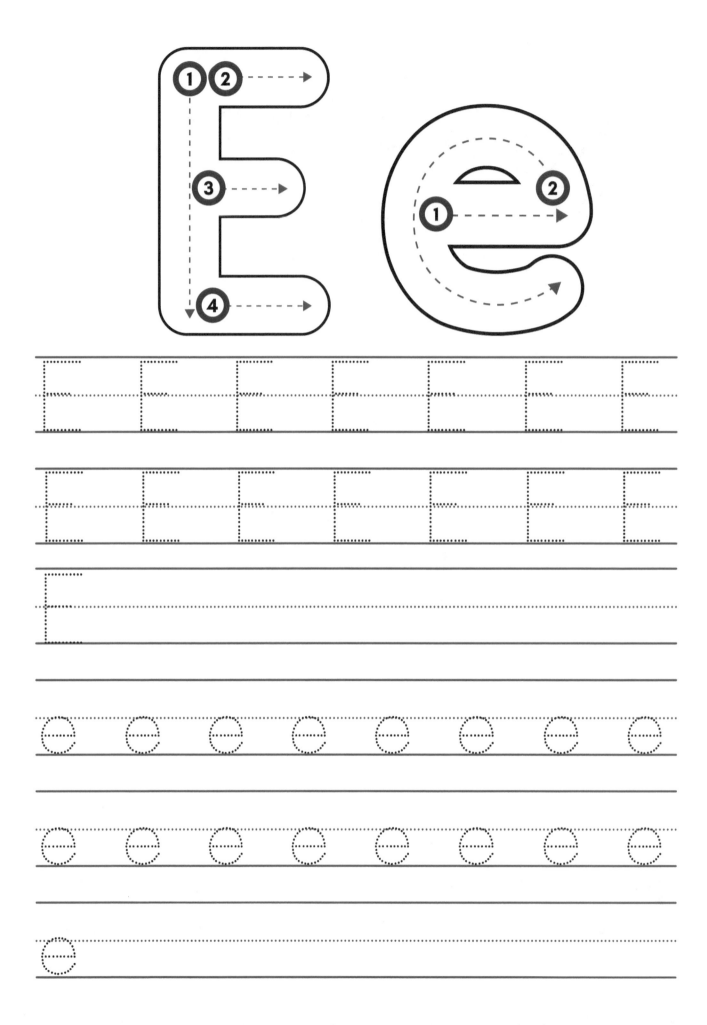

ever ever ever

ev

empire empire empire

em

echo echo echo

ec

eek eek eek

ee

Elephants eat
eggs everyday
in elevators.

write it on
your own

E

eg

in

more
practice

Take a break!

Letter E Actions

Empty all the trash cans in the house.

Explore the house like a pirate.

Erupt like a volcano.

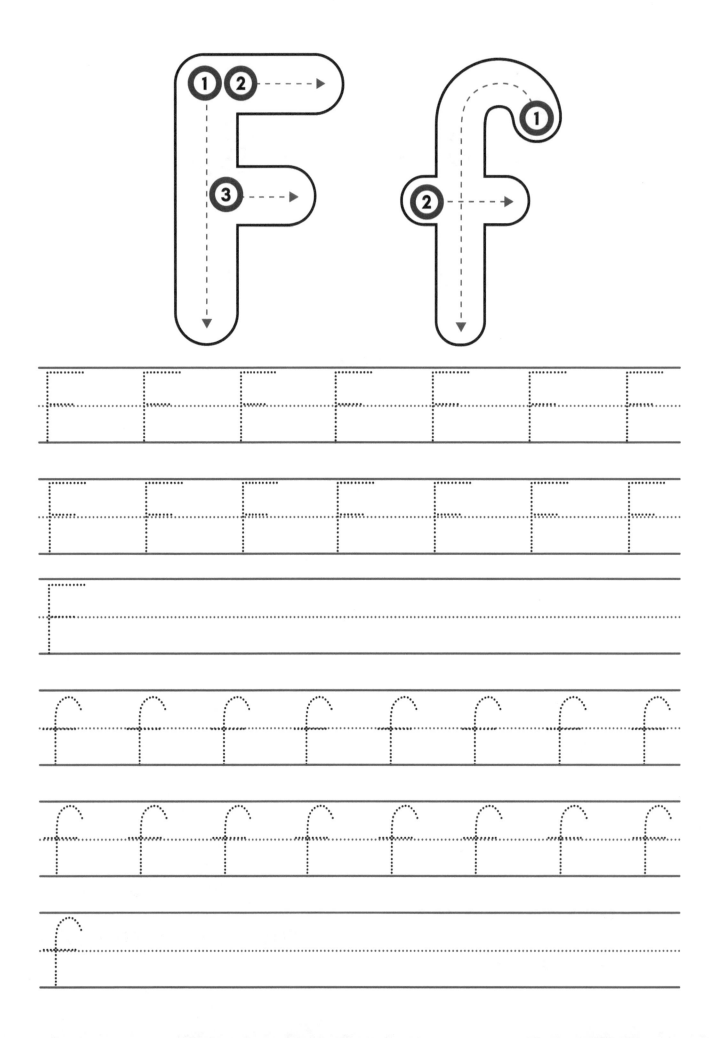

fix fix fix fix

fi

feed feed feed

fe

fill fill fill fill

fi

float float flat

fi

Foxes with fat,

fluffy tails

flee faster.

write it on
your own

Fo

fl

fl

more
practice

Take a break!

Letter F Actions

"Fly" around the room.

Flip your legs back over your head.

Flip and flop like a fish.

gift gift gift

gi

growl growl

gr

gutter gutter

gu

green green

gr

Guys grab
growling gators
and gallop!

write it on
your own
Gu

gr

an

more
practice

Take a break!

Letter G Actions

Growl like a lion
looking for lunch.

Go backwards
around the room.

Grab your feet with your
hands and walk around.

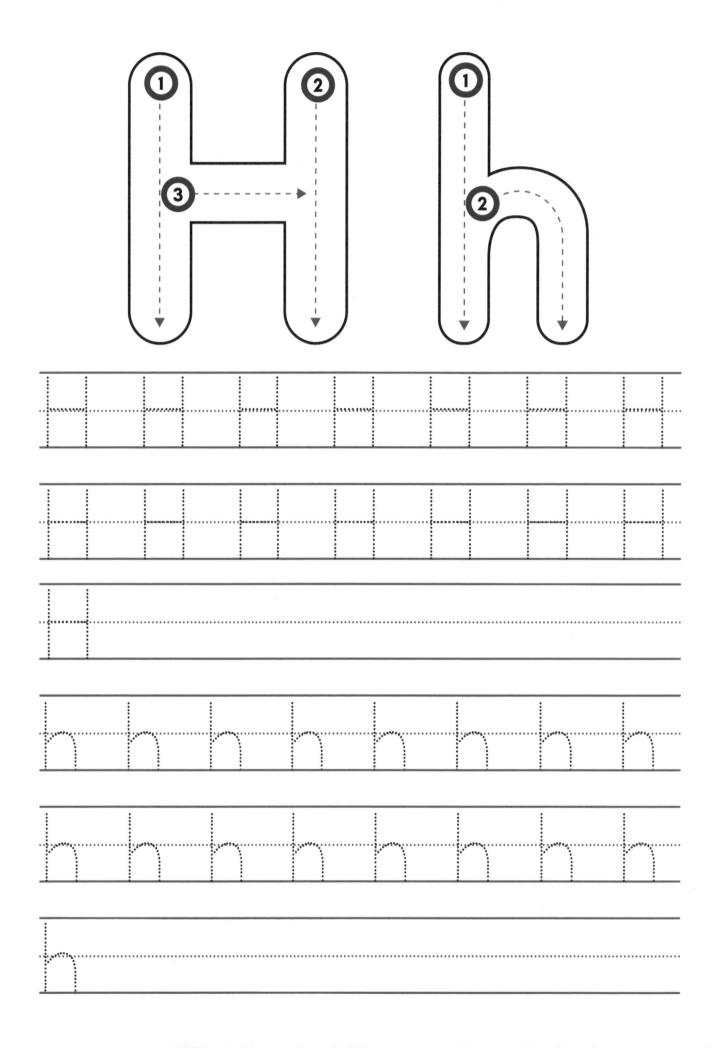

hello hello hello

he

huge huge huge

hu

hole hole hole

ho

home   home

ho

Happy hippos
hop on high
hydrangea
bushes.

write it on
your own

Ha

ho

hy

bu

Take a break!

Letter H Actions

Hop like a frog.

Hip hop dance.

Hop on one foot across the room.

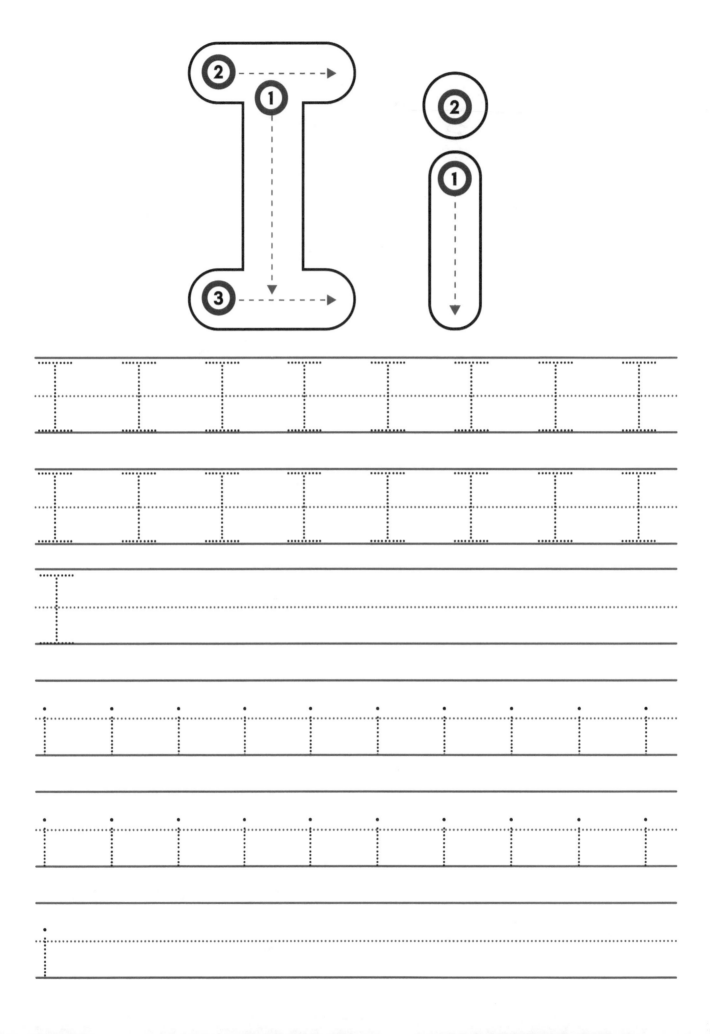

itchy itchy itch

it

Indian Indian

In

ink ink ink ink

in

I'm I'm I'm

I

Icky, sticky
ice cream on
igloos is
interesting.

write it on
your own

Ic

ic

ig

in

Take a break!

Letter I Actions

Inch around like
an inchworm.

Invent a new
gymnastics move.

Impress someone with
an awesome skill.

jump jump jump

ju

jet jet jet jet

je

jig jig jig jig

ji

joke joke joke

jo

Jolly jaguars juggle juicy, jelly donuts.

write it on your own

Jo

ju

je

more practice

Take a break!

Letter J Actions

Jump as far as you can in one leap.

Jump for as long as you can.

Juggle something.

king   king   king

ki

kilt   kilt   kilt   kilt

ki

koala   koala

ko

kin   kin   kin   kin

ki

Kind kangaroos

knit cool khaki

knickers.

write it on
your own

Ki

kn

kn

more
practice

Take a break!

Letter K Actions

Kick your legs up as high as you can.

Keep your eyes closed and see how long you can walk before bumping into something.

Knock on different things in the room to see how they sound differently.

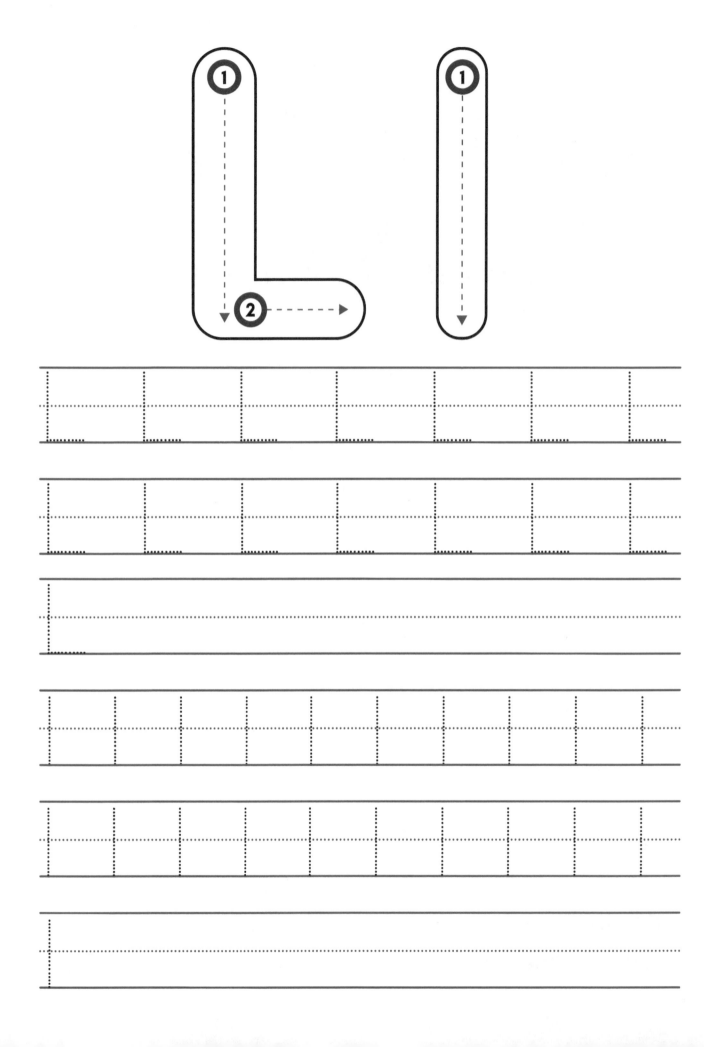

lump lump lump

tu

lost lost lost

to

long long long

to

legs legs legs

te

Llamas limp

after they leap

over lemons.

write it on your own

Ll

af

ov

more practice

Take a break!

Letter L Actions

Laugh out loud for as long as you can.

Leap like a deer.

Lower yourself down to the ground on one foot.

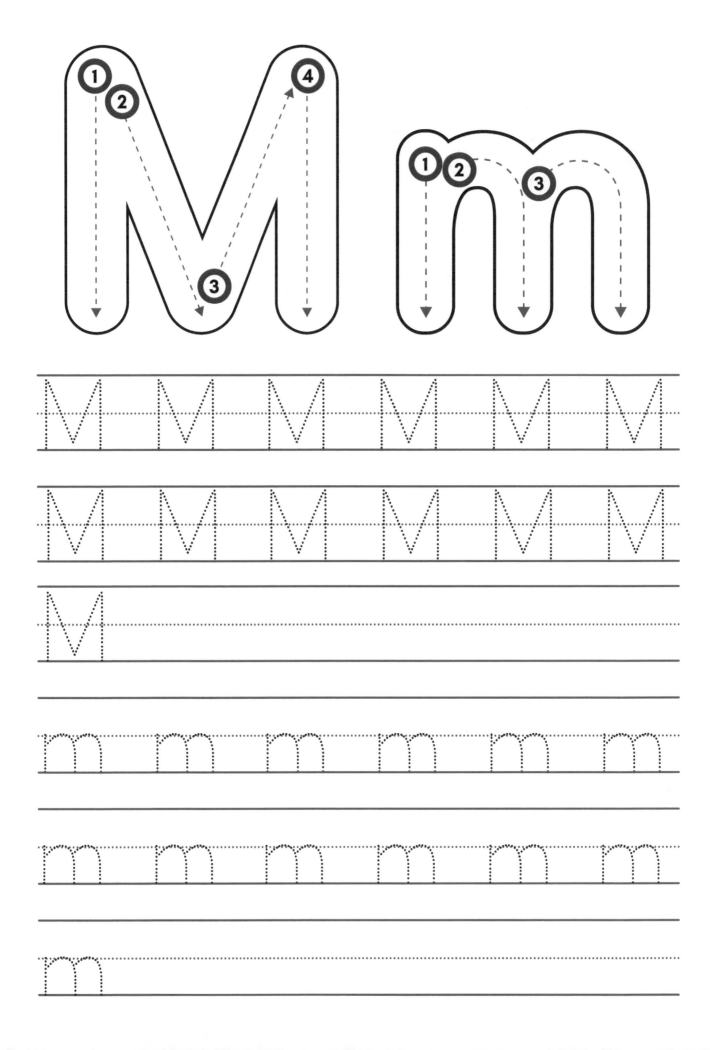

Mom Mom Mom

Mo

mice mice mice

mi

movie   movie

mo

mummy mummy

mu

Magic moose

make music in

the morning.

write it on
your own

Ma

ma

th

more
practice

Take a break!

Letter M Actions

Make a silly face.

March around the room like a soldier.

Mimic your favorite animals.

nerd nerd nerd

ne

nice nice nice

ni

neck neck neck

ne

nest nest nest

ne

Ninjas never

eat nasty,

neon nachos.

write it on
your own

Ni

ea

ne

more
practice

Take a break!

Letter N Actions

Neigh like a
bucking bronco.

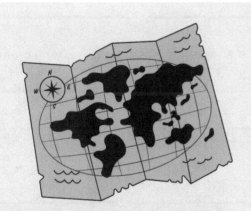

Navigate a trail
through the house.

Nod your head slowly
and then faster.

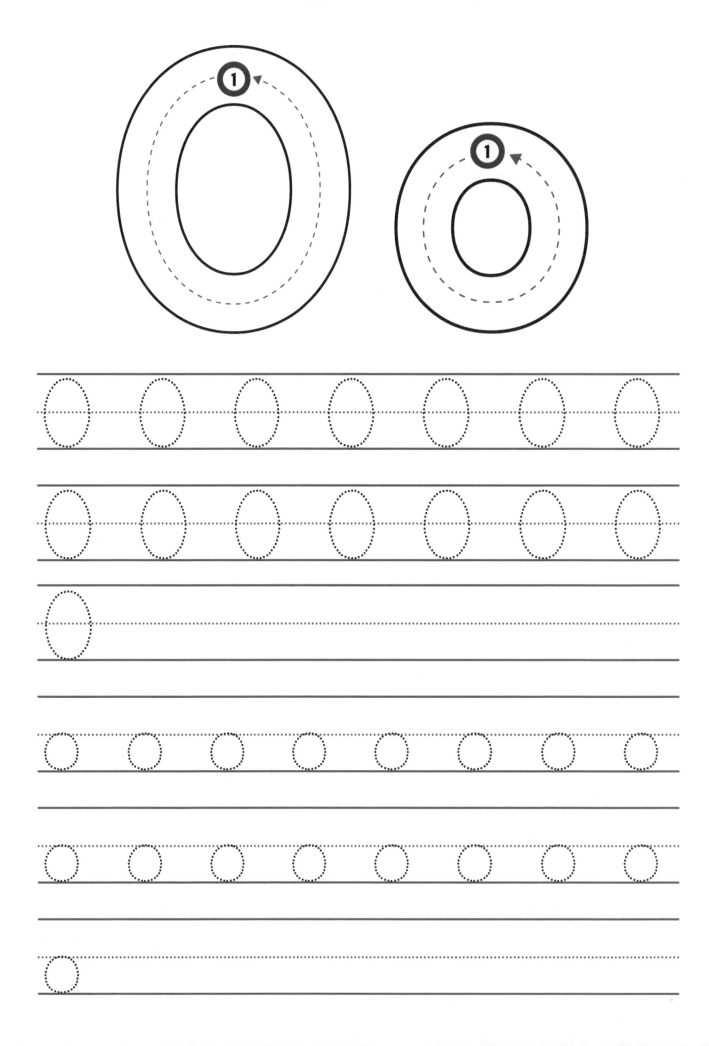

owl　　owl　　owl

ow

ox　ox　ox　ox

ox

over over over

ov

ooze ooze ooze

oo

Octopuses oink
and eat sour
oranges only.

write it on
your own

Oc

an

or

more
practice

Take a break!

Letter O Actions

Open and close your arms wide like a crocodile.

Open your mouth wide and shut it 10 times.

Organize your toys in a new way.

pop   pop   pop

po

pig   pig   pig

pi

puppy   puppy

pu

puke   puke   puke

pu

People eat

purple pickles

at every party.

write it on
your own

Pe

pu

at

more
practice

Take a break!

Letter P Actions

Pretend to be a panther stalking its prey.

Perform your favorite song.

Play like you're a cowboy.

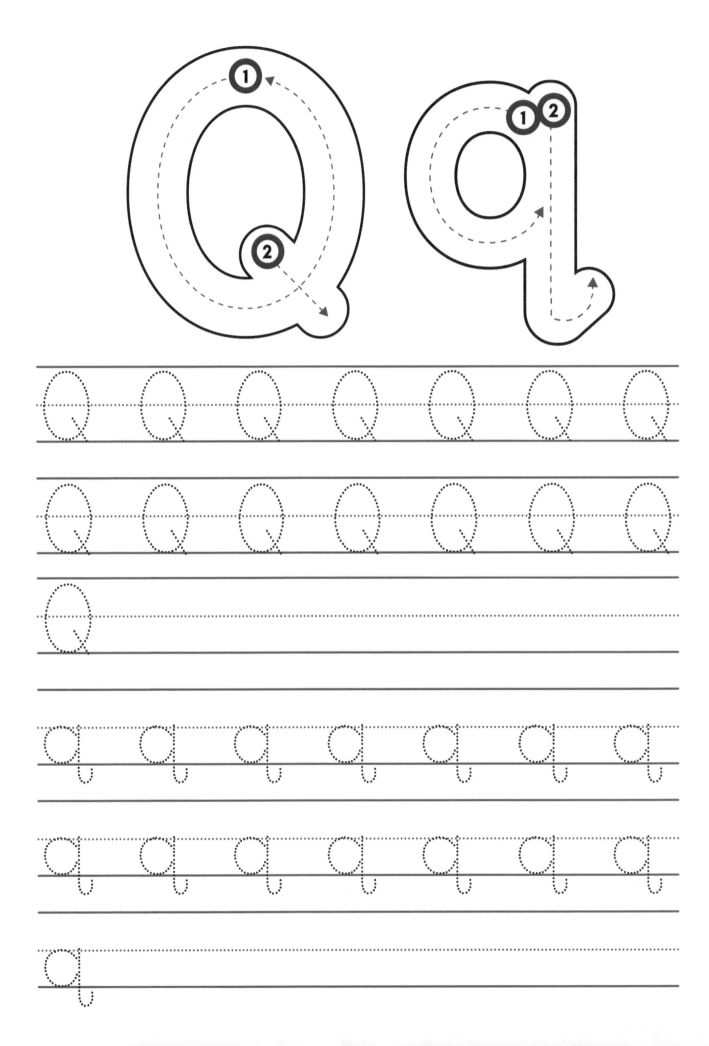

quick   quick

qu

quote   quote

qu

quirky   quirky

qu

quest   quest

qu

Quietly the

queen quit

quacking.

write it on
your own

Qu

qu

Qu

more
practice

Take a break!

Letter Q Actions

Quack like a duck while waddling around.

Quietly act like a dinosaur.

Quake and quiver all over.

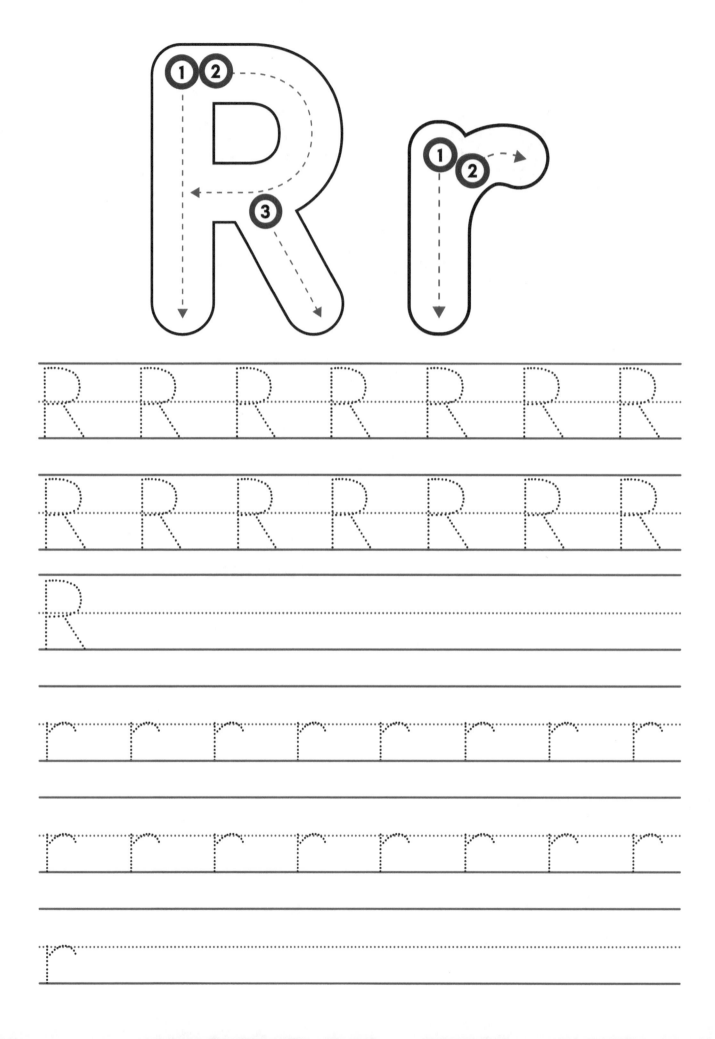

red red red

re

roar roar roar

ro

risk risk risk

ri

run run run run

ru

Rabbits race
to eat radishes
and rutabagas.

write it on
your own

Ra

to

an

more
practice

Take a break!

Letter R Actions

Repair something that's broken.

Race to another room as fast as you can.

Run backwards around the room five times.

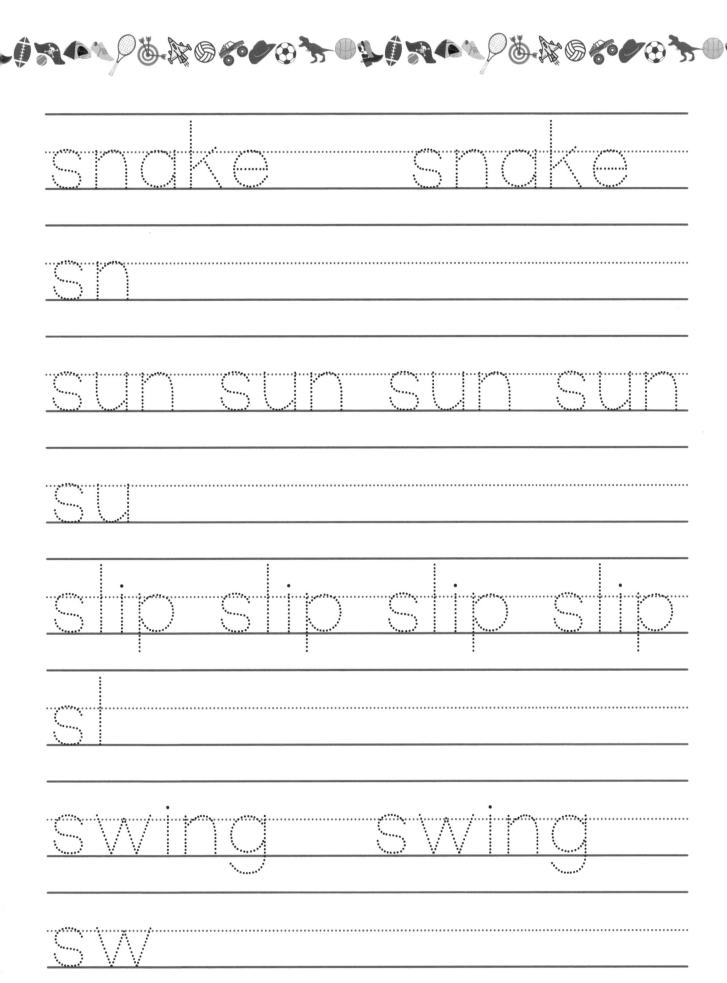

snake   snake

sn

sun sun sun sun

su

slip slip slip slip

sl

swing   swing

sw

Slimy snails sit
on the shore in
their seashells.

write it on
your own

Sl

on

th

more
practice

Take a break!

Letter S Actions

"Sail" around the
house like a boat.

Snore loudly while
pretending to sleep.

Scratch your head,
ears, nose, arms, feet,
and back.

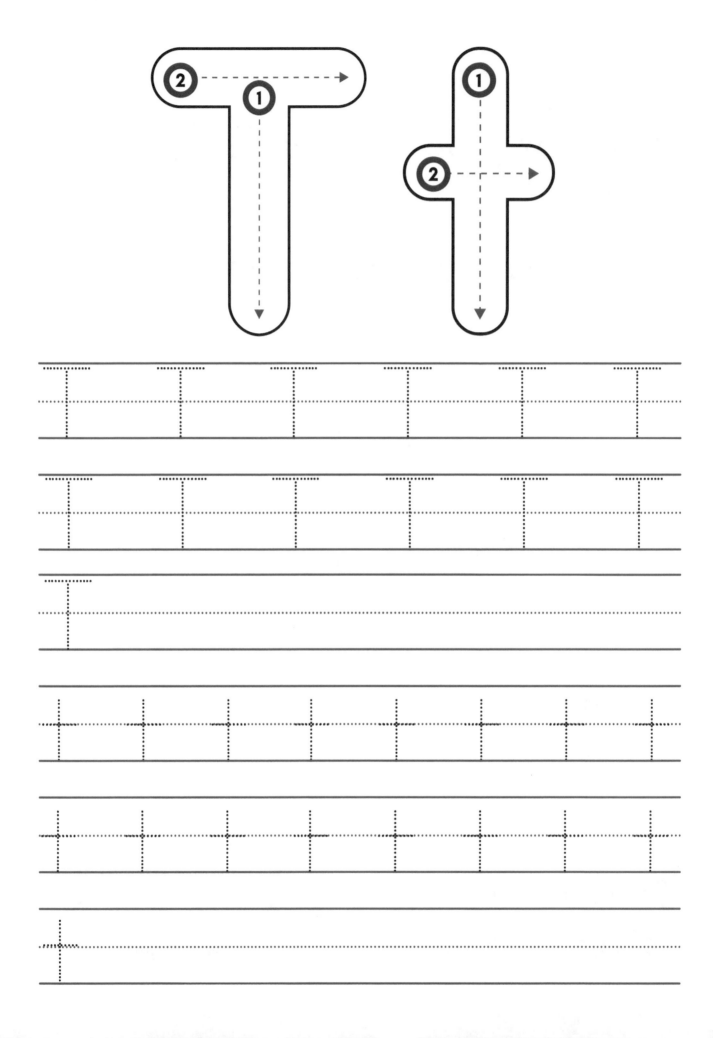

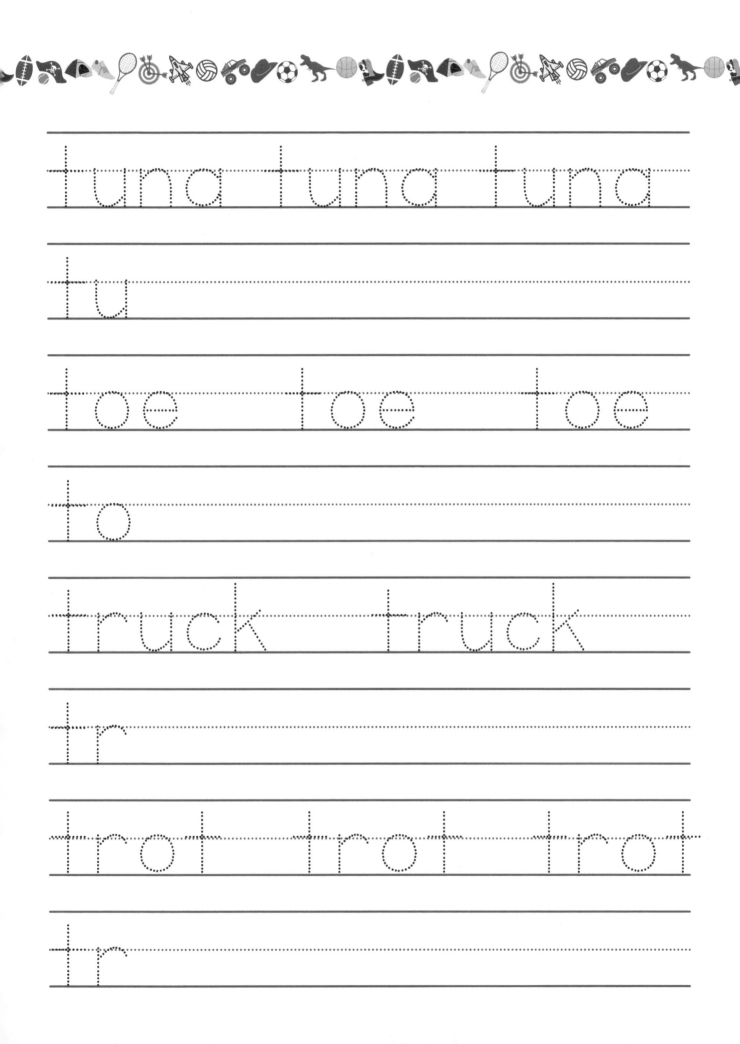

tuna tuna tuna

tu

toe   toe   toe

to

truck   truck

tr

trot trot trot

tr

Tickle the tiny
turtle and tap
its shell on top.

write it on
your own

Ti

tu

it

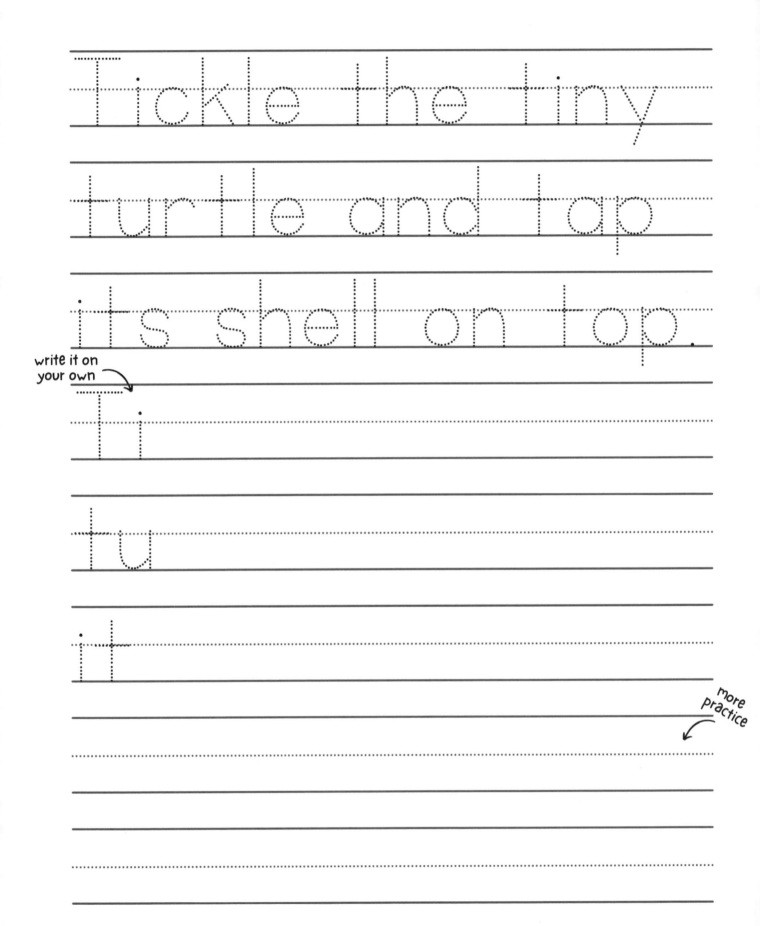

more
practice

Take a break!

Letter T Actions

Tip toe quietly around the room.

Turn around in circles till you feel dizzy.

Trot like a pony in a pasture.

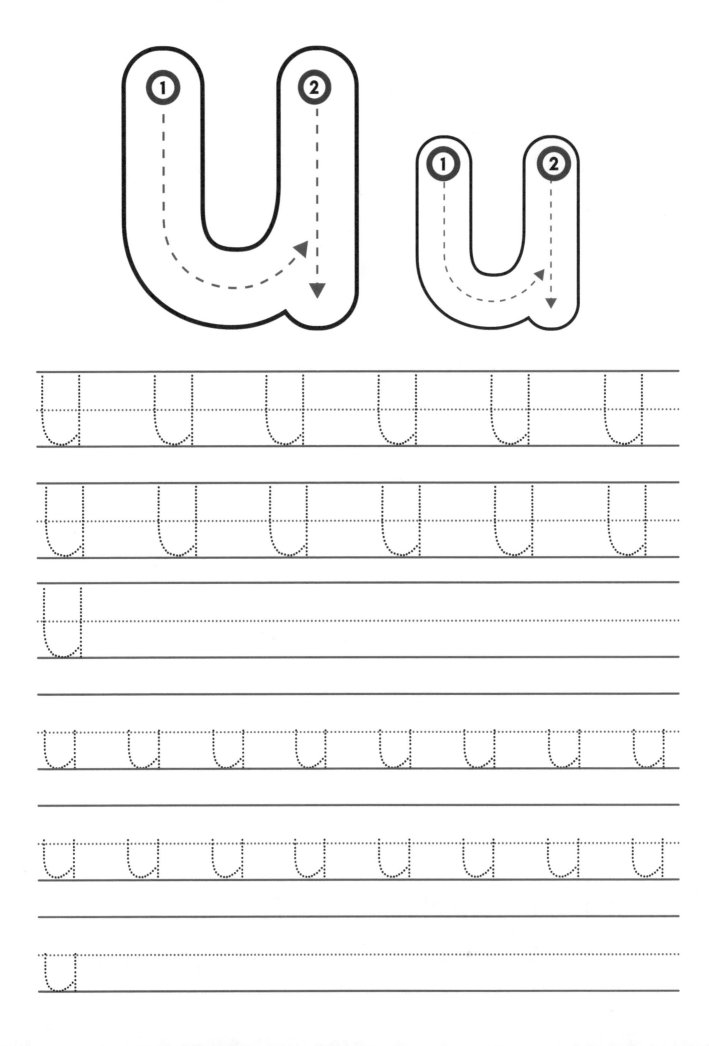

up up up up up

up

ukulele ukulele

uk

unicorn unicorn

un

use use use use

us

Uncle is under

the utterly ugly

umbrella.

write it on
your own

Un

the

um

more
practice

Take a break!

Letter U Actions

Unlock some things with your "invisible" key.

Untie all your shoes and tie them again.

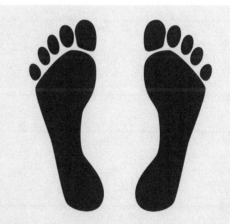

Use your feet to pick things up and move them.

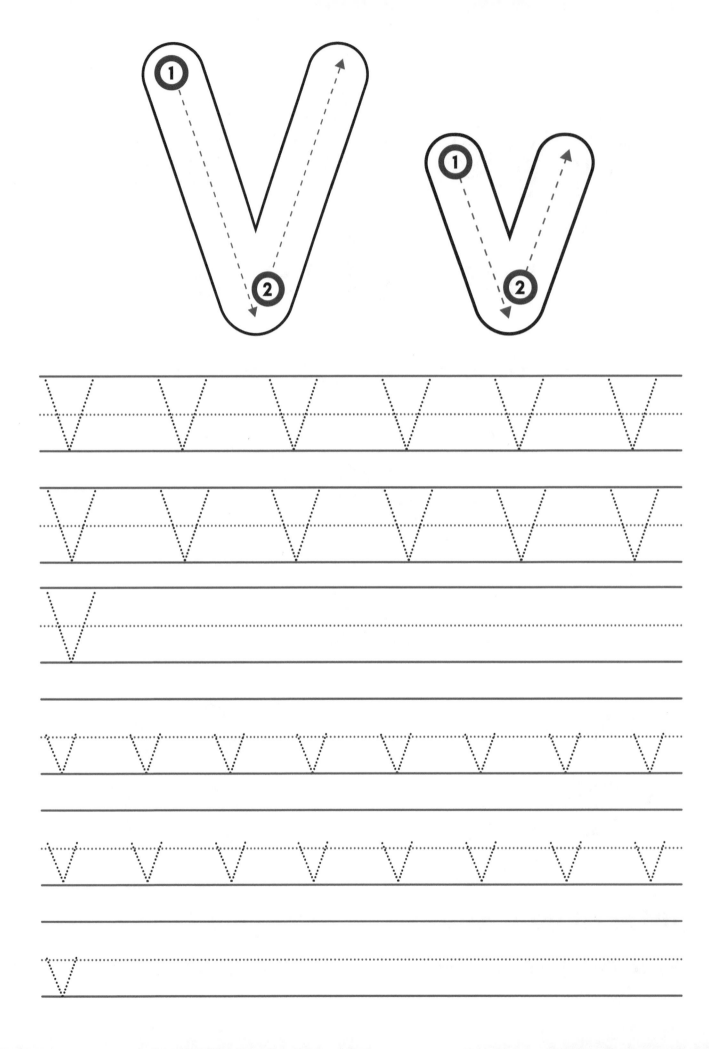

violin   violin

vi

veto veto veto

ve

volume   volume

vo

voice   voice

vo

Victor lives in
the village in
the valley.

write it on
your own

Vi

th

th

more
practice

Take a break!

Letter V Actions

"Vacuum" the floor while making loud vacuum noises.

Vanish from the room like you're in a magic act.

Vibrate your arms and legs very quickly.

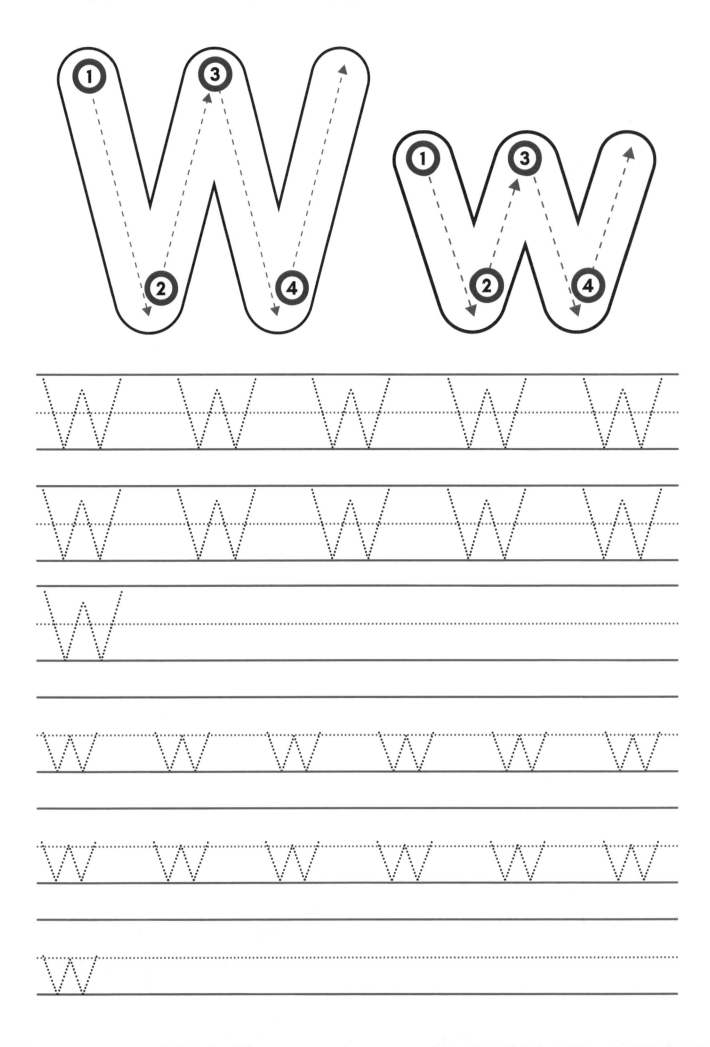

wow wow wow

wo

wet wet wet

we

wild wild wild

wi

wasp wasp

wa

Winter weather
blows west on
the weekends.

write it on
your own

Wi

bl

th

more
practice

Take a break!

Letter **W** Actions

Wash your whole body in a pretend bubble bath.

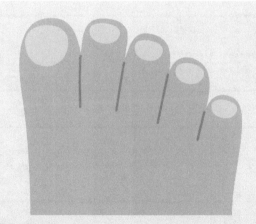

Wiggle your whole body starting with your toes.

Wander through the house looking for lost items.

x-ray   x-ray

x-

extra   extra

ex

X-mas   X-mas

X-

expert   expert

ex

X-ray the

X-mas gift to

see if it's

excellent.

write it on
your own

X-

X-

se

ex

Take a break!

Letter X Actions

"X-ray" one of your sick stuffed animals.

Exercise!

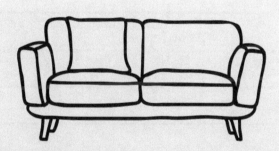

Examine the corners of the room and under the furniture to see what you can find.

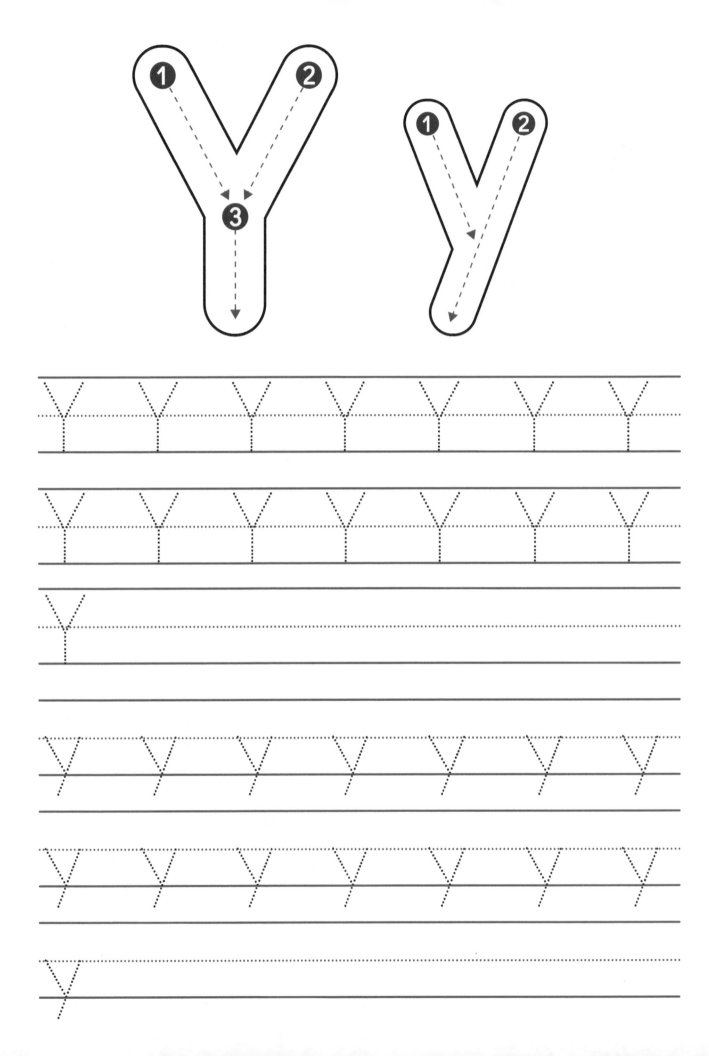

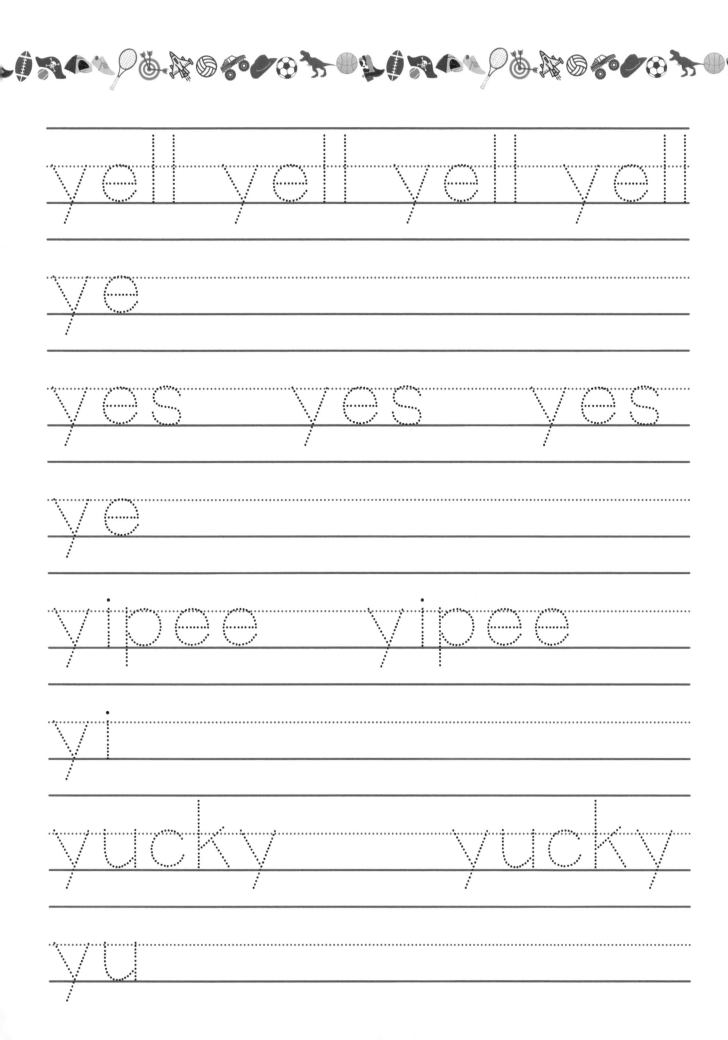

yell   yell   yell   yell

ye

yes   yes   yes

ye

yipee   yipee

yi

yucky   yucky

yu

Yodeling

youths yo-yo

on the yacht.

write it on
your own

Yo

yo

on

more
practice

Take a break!

Letter Y Actions

Yoga pose like this.

Yodel a loud tune.

Yap like an excited, little dog.

zip zip zip zip

zi

zoom   zoom

zo

zest zest zest

ze

zulu zulu zulu

zu

The zebra zigs and zebra zags on the zipline.

write it on your own

Th

an

th

more practice

Take a break!

Letter Z Actions

Zoom like a rocket
into outer space.

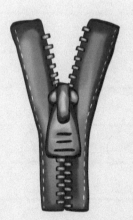

Zip and unzip something
fast 10 times.

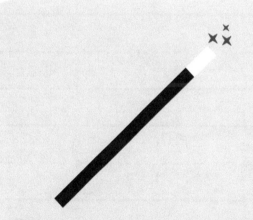

Zap someone with
your "magic wand."

NUMBERS

NUMBERS

4 4 4 4 4 4 4 4 4

5 5 5 5 5 5 5 5

6 6 6 6 6 6 6 6

7 7 7 7 7 7 7

NUMBERS

8 8 8 8 8 8 8

9 9 9 9 9 9 9

10 10 10 10 10

more practice

NUMBERS

zero   zero   zero

one   one   one

two   two   two

three   three

NUMBERS

four four four

five five five

six six six six

seven seven

NUMBERS

eight eight eight

nine nine nine

ten ten ten ten

more practice

FOR FUN!

Delicious ice cream and yummy hamburgers are way better than ice cubes and hominy. I am ready for the future!

If this page doesn't make sense, go back and read the note written to you at the beginning of this book. 😉

Made in United States
Troutdale, OR
06/20/2024

20692673R00064